USBORNE KEY SKILLS

Wipe-clean Weather and Seasons

Illustrated by Anna Süßbauer

Written by Holly Bathie

Designed by Keith Newell

Bun the rabbit

Coco the raccoon

spring

summer

Mo the mouse

Foxy the fox

autumn

winter

Series Editor: Felicity Brooks

Weather words

Spike enjoys taking photos around the wood. Below are some of the photos he has taken, and some weather words to describe them.

Draw lines to match each photo on this page to the words on this page that describe it. You could join more than one word to each photo.

hot sunny stormy

foggy dry windy

Now do the same for the photos on this page.

snowy cloudy wet

rainy cold icy

Weather symbols

A weather forecast tells you what the weather will be like. Hug is looking at the weather forecast for today.

Underline all the weather words in the forecast below.

It will be windy by the beach all day.

The lake will be sunny this afternoon.

It will rain over the harbour this morning.

There might be a thunderstorm over the sea tonight.

The forest will be cloudy this evening.

There is a chance of snow today.

Trace the weather symbols below for Hug.

thunderstorm

wind

rain

cloud

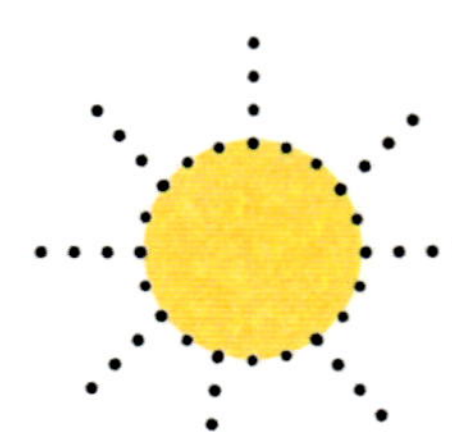

sun

Use the forecast to draw the weather symbols in the correct places on Hug's weather map.

Which symbol below do you think is the one for snow? Draw a ring around it for Hug.

Choose a place on the map where you think it will snow, then draw the snow symbol there.

Cloud spotting

Clouds can be different shapes, depending on the weather.

On a rainy day, the clouds are long and grey.

On a sunny day, the clouds are fluffy and white.

When it's about to thunder, tall clouds with a flat top appear.

Squilly and Spike are also cloud spotting.
The weather forecast says it's going to rain.
Draw some long, dark rain clouds in the sky.

Squilly

Spike

Now the sun has come out.
Draw it in the sky, and add
some fluffy white clouds.

Oh dear, a storm is coming!
Draw some tall thunderclouds
in the sky.

The four seasons

The four seasons of the year are: Spring, Summer, Autumn and Winter.

Draw lines to match the name of a season to each of the tree pictures below. Use the animals' signs to help you.

Spring Summer Autumn Winter

Some trees are green all year round, and don't lose their leaves. These are called 'evergreen' trees.

Look at these pictures and see if you can spot what changes with the seasons. Write the correct season name under each picture.

....

....

....

Spring rain

You can measure rainfall using a rain gauge.

How much rain is in the rain gauge?
Write the number in the box. ☐ cm

Foxy and Coco used the rain gauge to measure rainfall every day for four days. Fill in the boxes to show how much rain they collected each day in the rain gauge.

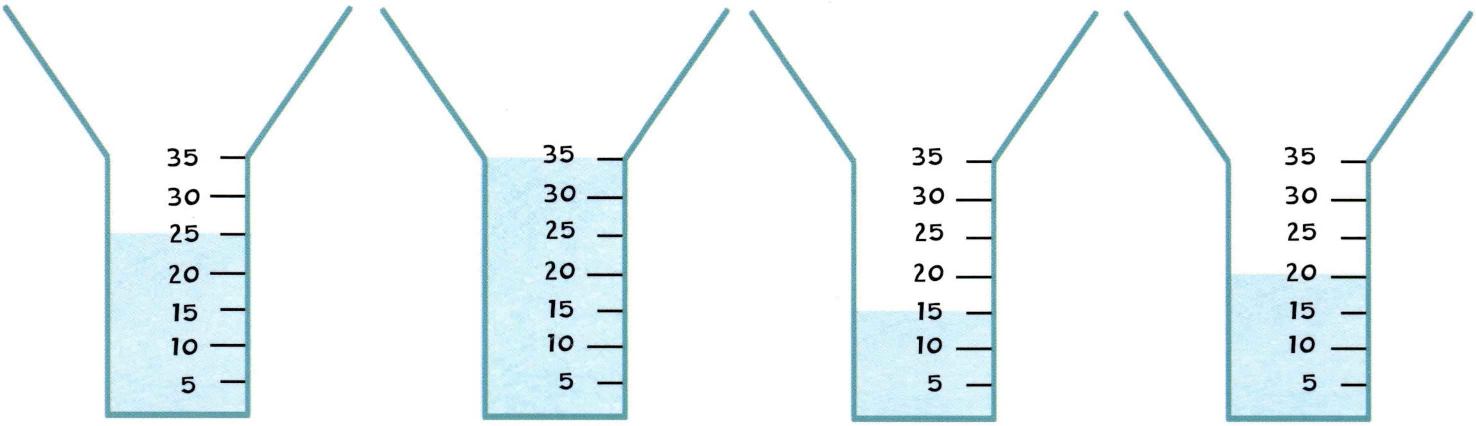

☐ cm	☐ cm	☐ cm	☐ cm
Monday	Tuesday	Wednesday	Thursday

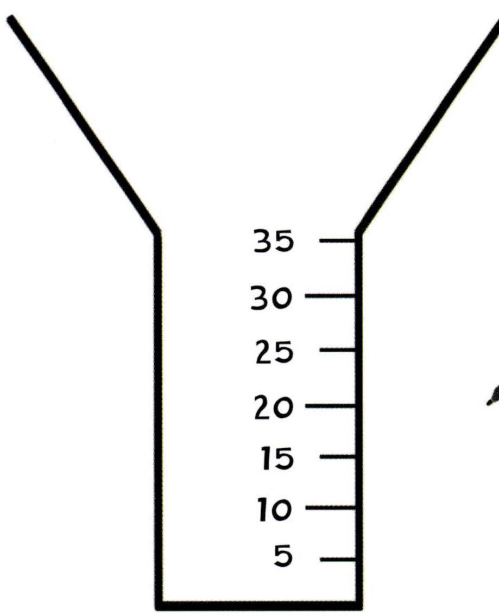

Shade in the empty rain gauge to show 5 cm of rain.

Now shade in the rain gauge to show 10 cm of rain.

Sun and shadows

A shadow is a dark shape that's made by something blocking the light. During the day, the sun moves across the sky, and as its light moves, the position of shadows changes.

morning | midday (lunchtime) | afternoon

These animals have all been for a walk in the sunshine today. Look at their shadows, then draw where the sun should be in each picture. One has been done for you.

morning | midday | afternoon

Now draw a line to match each time of the day to the right picture.

There are some shadows missing from Hug and Spike's afternoon picnic. Draw the shadows for two trees, the picnic basket, two bushes and the log.

Autumn wind

It's a lovely clear day in Wildflower Wood, and the animals have lots of fun planned.

A windsock shows how windy it is. Also, when there is some wind, it points in the direction the wind is blowing.

When there is no wind, there is no air in the sock, so it hangs down.

When it's a bit windy, air goes into the sock and lifts it up a little.

When there's a strong wind, the sock is out very straight, full of air.

The animals all need it to be a bit windy. Draw a wind sock on the striped pole on this page to show that it's a bit windy. Use Olly's guide on the opposite page to help you.

Now draw Spike, Stripe and Bun's kites flying in the direction your windsock is pointing.

Now draw the windsock pointing in the other direction, and draw the kites flying in the new direction of the wind.

Temperature

Temperature is a measure of how hot or cold it is.
A low temperature is cold, and a high temperature is hot.

Do you think the temperature is high or low in each picture below? Tick the right boxes.

high ☐

low ☐

high ☐

low ☐

high ☐

low ☐

high ☐

low ☐

You can measure the temperature using a thermometer.

The liquid in the bottom moves higher up the tube when it's hotter...

...and lower when it's colder.

The numbers are called 'degrees'. You can use a little sign like this after a number, to show degrees: °

Look at the number the liquid comes up to on the thermometers below. Fill in the boxes to show the temperatures.

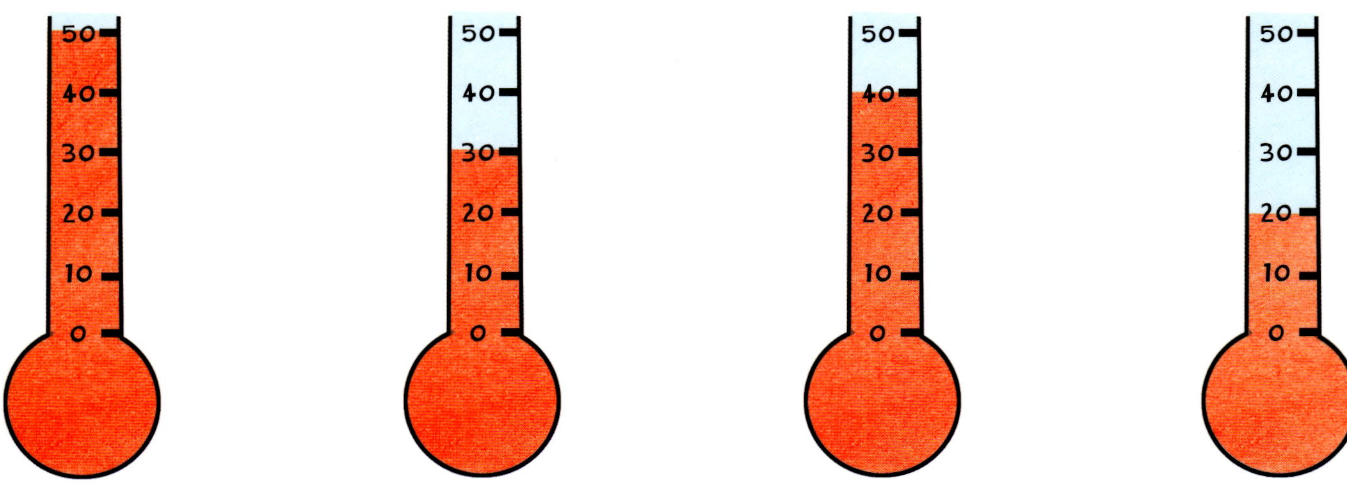

☐ ° ☐ ° ☐ ° ☐ °

Draw a triangle next to the lowest temperature.
Draw a square next to the highest temperature.

The seasons and daylight hours

These friends have made a chart showing the twelve months of the year. They have coloured the chart to show which season each month is in.

Key

- Spring (green)
- Summer (yellow)
- Autumn (red)
- Winter (blue)

Find the first month of the year and draw a star next to it.
Now draw a line to join the first month to the second month.

Keep joining the months up in order until you get to the last month of the year.

In Winter there are fewer hours of daylight than in the other seasons. It gets dark early in Winter, making the days short and the nights long.

In Summer there are more hours of daylight than in the other seasons, so it stays light past bedtime. The days are long and the nights are short.

Stripe and Bun have counted the hours of daylight in each month this year.

They've written each month and its hours of daylight in the chart below.

Jan	Feb	Mar	Apr	May	Jun	Jul	Aug	Sept	Oct	Nov	Dec
8	9	11	13	15	16	16	15	14	11	10	8

The friends have got stuck filling in their next chart. Write the missing numbers for them. Use the key on the opposite page, and the chart above, to help you.

Season	Hours of daylight		
Spring	11		15
Summer	16		
Autumn		11	
Winter		8	

Weather and seasons

Spike has recorded the weather and the number of daylight hours over five days this week.

The weather this week, by Spike

Monday	Tuesday	Wednesday	Thursday	Friday

8 hours	8 hours	8 hours	8 hours	9 hours

Which season do you think it is? Put a tick in the right box.

Spring ☐ Summer ☐ Autumn ☐ Winter ☐

Spike

Moley has done the same for another week.

The weather this week, by Moley

Monday	Tuesday	Wednesday	Thursday	Friday

15 hours	16 hours	16 hours	16 hours	16 hours

Which season do you think it is? Put a tick in the right box.

Spring ☐ Summer ☐ Autumn ☐ Winter ☐

Moley

Which season do you think each animal is dressed for?
Draw a line to match each animal to the correct sign.

Which season do you think your birthday is in?
Draw a circle around the right season sign, above.

Write your
name here: ....

Now draw a circle around the name of your birthday month, below.

January	February	March	April
May	June	July	August
September	October	November	December

Now write the name of your friend, or someone in your family, on the dotted line. Circle their birthday month and season.

Weather and seasons quiz

Find out how much you can remember about weather and seasons by doing this quiz. Answers on page 24.

A. Draw lines to join each weather symbol to the correct weather word.

wind thunderstorm cloud rain

B. Copy the name of the season into the space under the right picture.

Spring Summer Autumn Winter

....

....

....

....

C. Shade in each animal's rain gauge to show how much rain they have collected.

D. Shade in each animal's thermometer to show the temperature they are describing.

E. Hug has got the months of the year muddled up. He has put a '1' and a '12' above the first and last months. Help him by filling in the right number above each month, to order them from 1 to 12.

12 December

October

February

May

1 January

July

September

March

June

August

November

April

Quiz answers

A.

B.

Summer

Winter

Autumn

Spring

C.

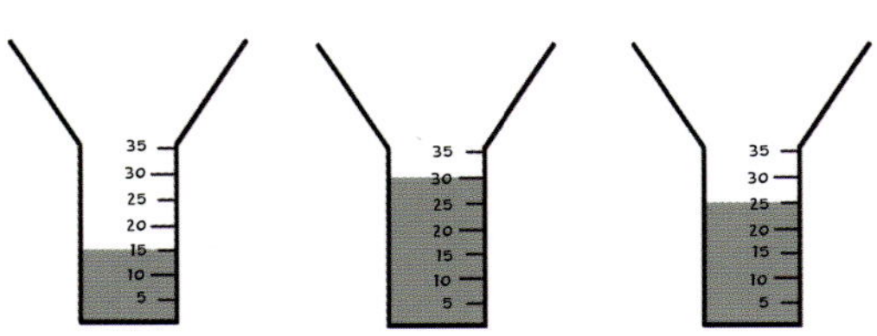

D.

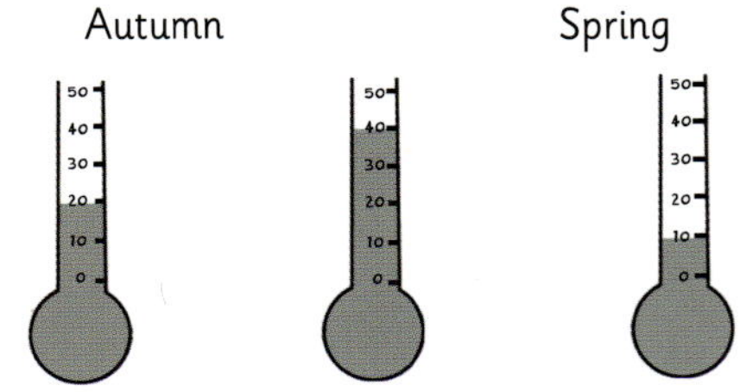

E. 1. January, 2. February, 3. March, 4. April, 5. May, 6. June, 7. July, 8. August, 9. September, 10. October, 11. November, 12. December.

Score 1 point for each correct answer and write your score in this box:
If you want to get a higher score, wipe the pages clean and try again.

____
24

The weather this week

Monday	Tuesday	Wednesday	Thursday	Friday	Saturday	Sunday

The rainfall this week, in centimetres

Monday	Tuesday	Wednesday	Thursday	Friday	Saturday	Sunday
cm	cm	cm	cm	cm	cm	cm

How I would describe the weather today...

Secret notes for grown-ups

Weather words (pages 2-3)
These pages help children to expand their vocabulary so that they can describe the weather. You could encourage them to describe the weather today, using some of these words.

Weather symbols (pages 4-5)
Using the 'weather this week' chart on the fold-out page, your child could choose and draw the appropriate weather symbol to record the weather each day for a week.

Cloud spotting (pages 6-7)
You and your child could try predicting if it might rain or thunder, based on the shape of the clouds outside. Perhaps children could make up their own weather forecast for the day.

The four seasons (pages 8-9)
When you are out on a walk with children, try to spot signs of the current season, including trees and their leaves, flowers, insects, animals, berries, nuts and seeds. In winter, children could spot evergreen trees.

Spring rain (pages 10-11)
You could help your child to make a rain gauge and measure rainfall for a week, using the chart on the fold-out page. Instructions can be found at the Usborne Quicklinks website below.

Sun and shadows (pages 12-13)
To help children understand how shadows move throughout the day, you could help your child to make a simple sundial. Instructions can be found at the Usborne Quicklinks website below.

Autumn wind (pages 14-15)
To observe how wind speed and direction can vary throughout the day, you could help your child to make a colourful windsock. Instructions can be found at the Usborne Quicklinks website below.

Temperature (pages 16-17)
You could discuss with children what items of clothing they might wear for high or low temperatures, and talk about whether the temperature feels high or low in each season.

The seasons and daylight hours (pages 18-19)
Encourage children to practise saying the months of the year out loud, in order. You could ask them 'Which month comes before...' and 'Which month comes after...'

Weather and seasons (pages 20-21)
To help children practise the activity on page 21, they could try guessing the birthday month of a friend or family member by asking you to describe the season, and any other events that occur in that month, to help them narrow it down.

Usborne Quicklinks

For links to websites where you can find out how to make a rain gauge, sundial and other simple weather instruments with your child, go to usborne.com/Quicklinks and type in the keywords 'key skills weather and seasons'. Children should be supervised online. Please follow the internet safety guidelines at the Usborne Quicklinks website.

Answers

page 2

These are some of the ways you could have described the photos:

Bun – foggy
Foxy – dry, hot, sunny
Mo – windy, stormy
Moley and Coco – stormy, windy

page 3

These are some of the ways you could have described the photos:

Stripe and Mo – cloudy
Bun and Mo – wet, cloudy, rainy
Squilly and Hug – cold, snowy, wet, icy
Mo – icy, cold, wet

pages 4-5

windy; sunny; rain; thunderstorm; cloudy; snow

This is the symbol for snow.

pages 8-9

Winter

Spring

Summer

Autumn

Pictures:

Mo – Winter
Bun – Winter
Hug – Autumn
Olly – Spring
Coco – Summer
Spike – Spring

pages 10-11

There is 30 cm of rain in the gauge.

Monday – 25 cm
Tuesday – 35 cm
Wednesday – 15 cm
Thursday – 20 cm

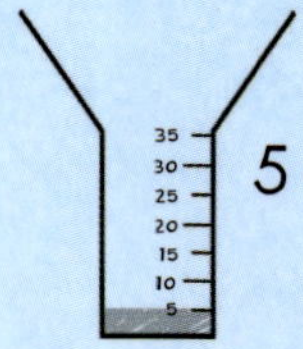

5 cm

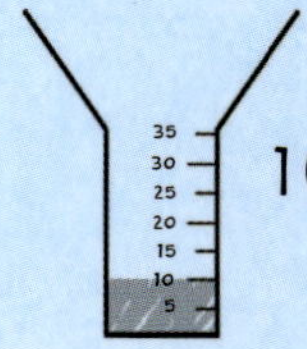

10 cm

pages 12-13

afternoon

morning

midday

pages 16-17

Pictures:

Mo and friend – high
Mo and Foxy – low
Spike – high
Mo and Stripe – low

■ 50°

30°

40°

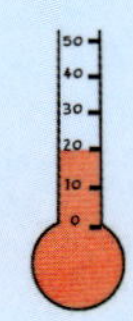
▲ 20°

pages 18-19

January–February–March–April–May–June–July–August–September–October–November–December

Season	Hours of daylight		
Spring	11	13	15
Summer	16	16	15
Autumn	14	11	10
Winter	8	8	9

pages 20-21

Spike: It's Winter
Coco – Summer
Stripe – Spring
Moley: It's Summer
Foxy – Winter
Hug – Autumn

USBORNE KEY SKILLS

Wipe-clean

Weather and Seasons

The Usborne Key Skills series supports and consolidates the Science that children learn at school and helps them develop and practise the essential skills they need to progress at each stage.

The activities in this book will build confidence in recognizing the characteristics of the different seasons, describing the weather and recording basic information.

£6.99
CAD$11.95

JFMAMJJASON /19
05338-1

CE

ISBN 978-1-4749-6525-5
9 781474 965255

WARNING! Not suitable for children under 36 months because of small parts. Choking hazard.

ATTENTION! Ne convient pas aux enfants de moins de 36 mois en raison des petites pièces. Risque de suffocation par ingestion.

usborne.com

Made with paper from a sustainable source.

Ink from pen may not be washable.
L'encre du feutre ne s'efface pas toujours au lavage.

First published in 2020 by Usborne Publishing Ltd., Usborne House, 83–85 Saffron Hill, London EC1N 8RT, England.
Printed in China.

Age 5 to
SCIENC

USBORNE KEY SKILLS